International Standard Book Nu:

A RICHARDS REFERENCE

Collections

MILITARY MONEY

BRITISH MILITARY AUTHORITY
(Including Tripolitania)

and

BRITISH ARMED FORCES

R. J. Marles © 1999 (and subsequently)

First Edition AD 2003

A compilation of averaged selling-prices drawn from dealers' lists, auctions and notaphily books and magazines.

ROTOGRAPHIC PUBLICATIONS · 37 St. Efrides Road
Torre · Torquay · TQ2 5SG · United Kingdom

ACKNOWLEDGEMENTS

This first edition is dedicated to Geoff Platt Esq., who erected the "sign post" which pointed the way to a fascinating series of special notes and vouchers; and to Steven Douglas-Brown Esq., who contacted the various Armed Forces authorities who might have, or might have had, an interest in the reproductions.

It is appropriate to thank all who helped, whether for a short telephone call or for lengthy correspondence. A long list risks leaving someone out, but there are some who specifically asked not to be mentioned. So, here is a "blanket" grateful thanks to all.

Sizes given follow steel rule measurement of actual notes (except for the few I couldn't get my hands on !). Variations are remarkably small. The reproductions are, in every instance, 70% of actual size.

For more information see foot-notes on page 23

PART ONE

British Military Authority · 6d, 1/-, 2/6d, 5/-, 10/-, £1 and the Z prefix overprints

PART TWO

British Military Authority in Tripolitania:
1 lira, 2 lira, 5 lira, 10 lira, 50 lira, 100 lira, 500 lira, and 1,000 lira.

PART THREE

Token coinage · N.A.A.F.I. TOKENS:

1/2 franc, 1 franc, 10 and 20 groschen, 1/4 piastre, 1/2 piastre, 5 and 10 lira, 1/2d (half-penny), 1d (one penny), half unit and one unit.

PART FOUR

British Armed Forces (BAFs):
First, Second, Third, Fourth, Fifth, Sixth (decimal) Series and 'Force T' notes.

PREFACE

(by Geoff Platt)

Although 'SIEGE NOTES' were produced in Khartoum in 1884/85 and in Mafeking in 1900, the first 'official' military issues were the British Treasury overprints for the Dardanelles Campaign at Gallipoli (Turkey), Iraq and Palestine in 1915. The current edition of *"Collectors Banknotes"* admirably details the military story. The two associated banknotes with their Arabic overprints for 60 and 120 silver piastres are listed under catalogue reference numbers RT15 (10 shillings) and RT34 (1 pound).

The Allies issued special paper money in 'Lira' for the invasion of Sicily and Italy in 1943. Similarly, 'Francs' were issued for the D-Day Landings in Normandy in 1944. The Lira issues were inscribed in English, whereas the Francs were printed with the phrase *Emis en France* (Issued in France) in deference to the fact that the Allies were liberating rather than invading. Allied notes were also issued for use in Germany and Austria respectively after these countries were invaded. During the blockade of Malta in 1941/42, a stock of old Maltese King George Vth 2/- notes, dated 1918, was *overprint surcharged* 1/- and put into circulation until small coinage could be obtained from England.

In Burma (now Myanmar) two types of overprint on Indian notes were circulated. Overprints also existed in Hong Kong and Malaya.

The above are outside the range of this book but, because of the British military association, might well become the subjects for future investigation and listing.

PART ONE
BRITISH MILITARY AUTHORITY

6d · 114 x 60mm
Lilac · Brown
Undated
Metal Thread
Lion-on Crown

RM1 (Pick M1)
(SB 301)

	V.F.	E.F.	Unc.
RM1	£12	£24	£36

1/- · 114 x 73mm
Grey · Violet
Undated
Metal Thread
Lion-on Crown

RM2 (Pick M2)
(SB 302)

	V.F.	E.F.	Unc.
RM2a	£5	£18	£35
2b letter X			
(West 98)		'X'	£125
2s specimen	---	---	£125

BRITISH MILITARY AUTHORITY 5

2/6d · 114 x 73mm
Green · Pink
Undated
Metal Thread
Lion-on Crown

RM3 (Pick M3)
(SB 304)

	V.F.	E.F.	Unc.
RM3a	£10	£20	£40
3b letter X		£60	---
3s specimen	---	---	---

5/- · 114 x 73mm
Maroon · Blue
Undated
Metal Thread
Lion-on Crown

RM4 (Pick M4)
(SB 304)

	V.F.	E.F.	Unc.
RM4a	£10	£20	£30
4b letter X		£60	£125
4s specimen	---	---	£125

BRITISH MILITARY AUTHORITY

RM5 (Pick M5)(SB 305) TEN SHILLINGS · 138 x 77.5mm
Blue/Olive (lilac tint) · Thread · Watermark (head of Athena)
Numbered top right and bottom left

	Fine	V.F.	E.F.	Unc.
RM 5 (Pick M5)(SB 305)	£7	£14	£40	£75
5b letter X (possibly)	--	---	---	---
5s specimen (noted 1997)		---	£185	---
5s specimen (noted 1998)		---	£220	£350
(noted 1999) 003/000 000			"Unc"	£150

BRITISH MILITARY AUTHORITY 7

RM6 (Pick M6)(SB306)   ONE POUND · 152 x 85mm
Violet/Orange (greenish tint) · Thread · Watermark (head of Athena)
Numbered top right and bottom left

	Fine	V.F.	E.F.	Unc.
RM 6 (Pick 6)(SB306)	£16	£25	£50	£90

★ *See, also, pages 8 and 9* ★

BRITHSH MILITARY AUTHORITY

RM6b · BULGARIA overprint

IMP

RM6c · FRANCE overprint

						Fine	V.F.	E.F.	Unc.
RM	6b	overprint	BULGARIA	(Z)	25 made	- -	- - -	£875	£1,200
	6c	overprint	FRANCE	(Z)	50 made	- -	- - -	£1,200	- - -
	6d	overprint	GREECE	(Z)	25 made	- -	- - -	- - -	- - -

★ See, also, pages 6 and 7 ★

BRITISH MILITARY AUTHORITY 9

IMP

RM6d · GREECE overprint

RM6sp · back of perforated specimen

	Fine	V.F.	E.F.	Unc.
★ See, also, pages 6 and 7 ★				
RM 6e letter X	£30	£60	£120	£200
6sb specimen twice in black	- -	- - -	- - -	£450
6sp specimen twice in perforations	- -	- - -	- - -	£500

PART TWO
BRITISH MILITARY AUTHORITY: TRIPOLITANIA

1 LIRA · 111 x 58mm
Green · Olive tint
Not numbered
Thread
Lion-on Crown

RM10
(Pick Libya M1)(SB 321)

	V.F.	E.F.	Unc.
RM10	£3	£8	£12
10s specimen	---	---	£50

SPECIMEN in red at top and bottom where applicable

2 LIRA 111 x 58mm
Blue · Green
Not numbered
Thread
Lion-on Crown

RM11
(Pick Libya M2)(SB 322)

	V.F.	E.F.	Unc.
RM11	£8	£20	£35
11s specimen	---	---	£130

BRITISH MILITARY AUTHORITY: TRIPOLITANIA 11

5 LIRA 114 x 58mm
Green · Reddish tint
Not numbered
Thread
Lion-on Crown

RM12
(Pick Libya M3)(SB 323)

	V.F.	E.F.	Unc.
RM12	£6	£16	£28
12s specimen	---	---	£100

10 LIRA 114 x 73mm
Lilac · Green tint
Not numbered
Thread
Lion-on Crown

RM13
(Pick Libya M4)(SB 324)

	V.F.	E.F.	Unc.
RM13	£10	£15	£25
13s specimen	---	---	£100

12 BRITISH MILITARY AUTHORITY: TRIPOLITANIA

50 LIRA 114 x 72mm
Yellow-Brown
Not numbered
Thread
Lion-on-Crown

RM 14
(Libya PM5)(SB 325)

        V.F. E.F. Unc.
RM14   £15 £45 £65
14s specimen - - - £200

100 LIRA 114 x 72mm
Orange · Grey tint
Not numbered
Thread
Lion-on-Crown

RM 15
(Libya PM6)(SB 326)

        V.F. E.F. Unc.
RM15 £15 £75 £100
15s specimen - - - £260

BRITISH MILITARY AUTHORITY: TRIPOLITANIA 13

RM 16 (Libya PM7) (SB 327)   500 LIRA · 139 x 77mm
Green · Blue tint · Thread · Watermark (head of Athena)
Numbered top right

	V.F.	E.F.	Unc.
RM 16	£45	£200	£450
16s specimen	---		£600

RM 17 (Libya PM8) (SB 328)   1000 LIRA · 150 x 85mm
Blue · Brown tint · Thread · Watermark (head of Athena)
Numbered top right

	V.F.	E.F.	Unc.
RM 17	£65	£300	£650
17s specimen		---	£850

Specimen set: 5, 10, 50, 100, 500 and 1,000 Lira
offered at auction (Spink 1998) "Unc." £2,200/£2,400

PART THREE
TOKENS (N.A.A.F.I. TOKENS)

"French" NAAFI on a plastic known as CP3 (Formica/Laminex)

			V.F.	E.F
RMT 1	1/2 franc · octagonal · brown · struck incuse	24mm	£10	£15
RMT 2	1/2 franc · 0.5mm letters · printed	24mm	£6	£10
RMT 3	1/2 franc · 1.5mm letters · printed	24mm	£4	£8

RMT 4	1/2 franc · 2.5mm letters · printed	24mm	£2	£5
RMT 5	ONE FRANC · ?		---	---

"Austrian" NAAFI on coloured plastic

RMT 6	10 groschen · hexagonal · yellow	25mm	£9	£14

RMT 7	20 groschen · hexagonal · red	25mm	£9	£14
RMT 8	1/4 piastre · EGYPT ONLY · round · red	22mm	£12	£20

RMT 9	1/4 piastre · SUDAN ONLY · round · red	22mm	£40	£60
RMT 10	1/2 piastre (presumed) no value shown · green	26mm	£10	£17

Schwan & Boling indicate that the 1/4 piastre was used in Cyprus as 1 mil and the 1/2 piastre used in the Maldives as 1 penny.

TOKENS (N.A.A.F.I. TOKENS) 15

"Italian" NAAFI · Sardinia Air Base

			V.F.	E.F
RMT 11	5 lira · aluminium · round · uniface	23mm	- - -	- - -
RMT 12	10 lira · aluminium · round · uniface	29mm	- - -	- - -

BRITISH ARMED FORCES

			Fine	V.F.	E.F.
RMT 13	1/2d · CP3 · round · brown	25mm	£4	£10	£22
RMT 14	1d · CP3 · round · brown	29mm	£4	£10	£22

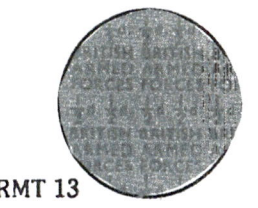 

RMT 13   RMT 14

Strictly SERIES 3 but listed to keep tokens together

RMT 15	HALF UNIT · brass · holed	20mm	£15	£40	£75
RMT 16	ONE UNIT · brass · holed	25.5mm	£15	£40	£75

RMT 15   RMT 16

PART FOUR
BRITISH ARMED FORCES · First Series

THREEPENCE
114 x 57mm
Purple over Orange
No number
No Thread

RM 20 (PM9) (E-01)

	V.F.	E.F.	Unc.
RM 20	£8	£16	£30
RM 20b	£10	£20	£40

RM 20b · perforation cancelled diagonally

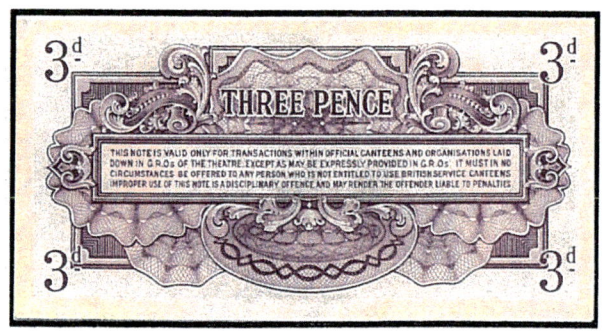

BRITISH ARMED FORCES · First Series 17

THREEPENCE
114 x 57mm

	V.F.	E.F.	Unc.
RM 21	£25	£40	£80
RM 21b	---	£200	---

RM 21 FORCE 'T' note
RM 21b local 'expedient'

> RM21 printed overprint:
> ISSUED IN HM SHIPS AFLOAT
> FOR USE IN
> NAAFI CANTEENS ONLY
>
> RM21b stamped overprint:
> ISSUED IN H.M. SHIPS
> FOR USE ONLY IN
> N.A.A.F.I. CANTEENS

RM 21 (PM9b) (E-08)

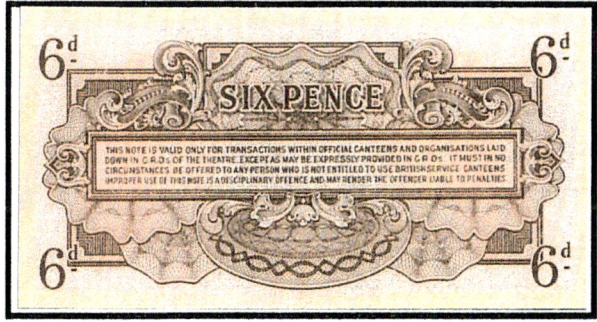

SIXPENCE
114 x 57mm
Brown/Red (blue tint)
No number
No Thread

Reverse

RM 22 (PM10) (E-02)   RM 22b similar to RM 20b

	V.F.	E.F.	Unc.
RM 22	£10	£20	£40
RM 22b	£12	£25	£50
RM 23a	£18	£32	£60
RM 23b	£25	£60	£125

RM 23 FORCE 'T' note
RM 23b local 'expedient'   **RM 23** (PM10a) (E-09)   RM 23b similar to RM 21b

BRITISH ARMED FORCES · First Series

One Shilling
114 x 57mm
Blue (Green/Orange)
No number
No thread

RM 24 (PM11) (E-03)

	V.F.	E.F.	Unc.
RM 24	£15	£25	£45
RM 24b	£20	£35	£65

RM 24b
perf. cancelled

RM 25 (PM11b) (E-10)

1/- · 114 x 57mm

	V.F.	E.F.	Unc.
RM 25	£30	£50	£90
RM 25b	£30	£50	£90
RM 25s (West)			£125

RM 25 FORCE 'T' note
RM 25b local 'expedient'
RM 25s specimen

RM 25 printed overprint:
ISSUED IN HM SHIPS AFLOAT
FOR USE IN
NAAFI CANTEENS ONLY

RM 25b stamped overprint:
ISSUED IN H.M. SHIPS
FOR USE ONLY IN
N.A.A.F.I. CANTEENS

BRITISH ARMED FORCES · First Series 19

RM 26 (PM12) (E-04)   Two Shillings and Sixpence
Red (Green tint) · no thread · Number at right 126 x 63
Reverse similar to that of the One Shilling

	V.F.	E.F.	Unc.
RM 26	£12	£18	£30
RM 26b perf. cancelled as RM 24b	---	£30	£60

RM 26 found with central thread   D/6 471948 uncancelled

RM 27 (PM12b) (E-11)   Two Shillings and Sixpence
Red (Green tint) · no thread · Number at right 126 x 63
Reverse similar to that of the One Shilling

	V.F.	E.F.	Unc.
RM 27 with Force 'T' overprint	£30	£60	£90
RM 27b with rubber stamp overprint	£30	£60	£90

BRITISH ARMED FORCES · First Series

RM 28 (PM13) (E-05)   Five Shillings
Green · No thread · Number at right · 126 x 63mm
Reverse similar to that of the Ten Shillings

	Fine	V.F.	E.F.	Unc.
RM 28	£12	£20	£40	£65
RM 28b perforation cancelled	---	---	£35	£60

RM 29 (PM13b) (E-12)   Five Shillings
Green · No thread · Number at right · 126 x 63
Reverse similar to that of the Ten Shillings

	Fine	V.F.	E.F.	Unc.
RM 29 with Force 'T' overprint	£15	£25	£75	£125
RM 29b rubber stamped overprint	---	---	£75	£125

BRITISH ARMED FORCES · First Series 21

RM 30 (PM14) (E-06)   Ten Shillings
Purple (Orange tint) · Thread · Numbers left and right · 139 x 70mm

		Fine	V.F.	E.F.	Unc.
RM 30a		£8	£18	£30	£45
RM 30b	perforation cancelled	---	---	£45	£60
RM 30b	(noted 2001)	"about unc"	---	---	£65

RM 31 (PM14b) (E-13)   Ten Shillings
Purple (Orange tint) · Thread · Numbers left and right · 139 x 70mm
Overprint similar to that of the Five Shillings

		V.F.	E.F.	Unc.
RM 31a	with Force 'T' overprint	£125	£200	£350
RM 31b	with rubber stamp overprint	£125	£200	£350

BRITISH ARMED FORCES · First Series

RM 32 (PM15) (E-07) One Pound
Blue (tints) · Thread · Numbers left and right · 139 x 70mm
Numbers printed in black

	Fine	V.F.	E.F.	Unc.
RM 32	£12	£18	£32	£60

RM 32b   perforation cancelled   ---   ---   £35   £75
Cancellation is diagonally using the word 'CANCELLED' spelt out by letters formed with perforations

RM 32s   A3 000000 specimen with oval DE La Rue stamp
(at auction)   £400

BACK

BRITISH ARMED FORCES · First Series

RM 33 (PM15a) (E-14) One Pound
Blue (tints) · Thread · Numbers left and right · 139 x 70mm
Numbers printed in black

	Fine	V.F.	E.F.	Unc.
RM 33a	£30	£90	£250	- - -

RM 33b stamped overprint not determined   - - -   - - -   - - -

---

For more information concerning many aspects of these fascinating military notes, you are directed to "WORLD WAR II REMEMBERED" by C. Frederick Schwan and Joseph E. Boling.

For even more (a vast amount of) detail, particularly the reasons for issuing the notes, their designs, secret marks etc., T. F. A. van Elmpt's "British Armed Forces SPECIAL VOUCHERS" is recommended.

Reminder: the PM numbers given alongside our own RM numbers refer to Volume Two EIGHTH Edition of "World Paper Money" by Albert Pick. The E numbers are those of van Elmpt, earlier referred to.

24   BRITISH ARMED FORCES · Second Series

RM 41 (PM16a) (E-15)   THREE PENCE
115 x 58mm · Brown (Pink/Green tints)
Security thread · no number

RM 42 (PM16b) (E-22)
as RM 41 but watermarked paper · no thread

			V.F.	E.F.	Unc.
RM	41		£3	£5	£9
	42	On watermarked paper · no thread	£2	£3	£6
	42s	Specimen · (at auction) "cancelled E.F." - -	- -	£200

BACK

BRITISH ARMED FORCES · Second Series

RM 43 (PM17) (E-16)   SIX PENCE
115 x 58mm · Deep Olive (Orange/Green tints)
Security thread · no number

RM 44 (PM17b) (E-23)
as RM 43 but watermarked paper · no thread

			V.F.	E.F.	Unc.
RM	43		£3	£5	£15
	44	On watermarked paper · no thread	£2	£3	£9
	44s	Specimen · (at auction) "cancelled E.F." - -	£200	- - - -

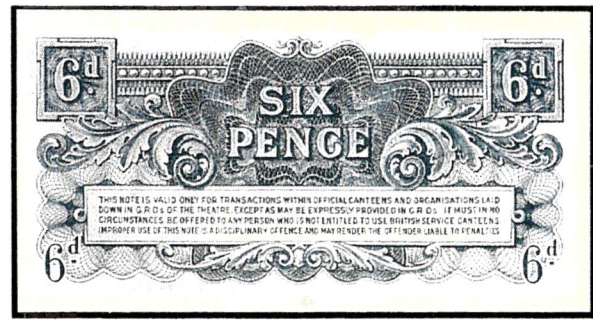

BACK

26   BRITISH ARMED FORCES · Second Series

RM 45 (PM18a) (E-17)   One Shilling

115 x 58mm · Red (Green/Purple tints)
Security thread · No number

RM46 (PM18b)(E-24)
as RM45 but watermarked paper · no thread

			V.F.	E.F.	Unc.
RM	45		£3	£6	£12
	46	On watermarked paper · no thread	£2	£4	£8
	46s	Specimen · perforation cancelled (at auction)	- -	- -	£200

BACK common to all three

BRITISH ARMED FORCES · Second Series

RM 47 (PM19a) (E-18)   Two Shillings Sixpence
128 x 63mm · Purple (Orange/Green tints)
Security thread · Numbered in Bright Red

RM 48 (PM19b) (E-25)
as RM47 but on watermarked paper · no thread
Numbered in Deep Maroon

			V.F.	E.F.	Unc.
RM	47		£3	£5	£15
	48	On watermarked paper · no thread	£2	£4	£12
	48s	Specimen · (O'Grady 1995) "E.F.+"	- -	£185	- - -

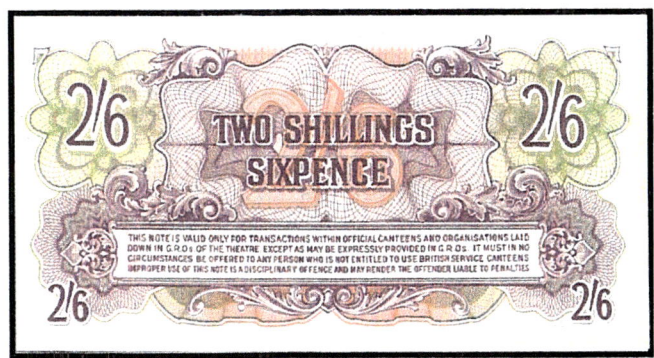

BACK common to all

BRITISH ARMED FORCES · Second Series

RM 49 (PM20a) (E-19)   Five Shillings
128 x 64· Blue (Orange/Red tints)
Security thread · Numbered in Bright Red

RM 50 (PM20b) (E-26)
as RM49 but watermarked paper · no thread
Numbered in Deep Maroon
CD/1s found numbered in both Bright Red and in Deep Maroon

		V.F.	E.F.	Unc.
RM 49	Plain paper · Security thread	£8	£12	£25
RM 50a	Watermarked paper · no thread	£6	£9	£20
RM 50b	Punch cancelled 2 holes	£3	£6	£15
RM 50s	Specimen · (O'Grady 1995) "E.F.+"	---	---	£185
RM 50s	Specimen · (noted 2001) "Unc."	---	---	£250

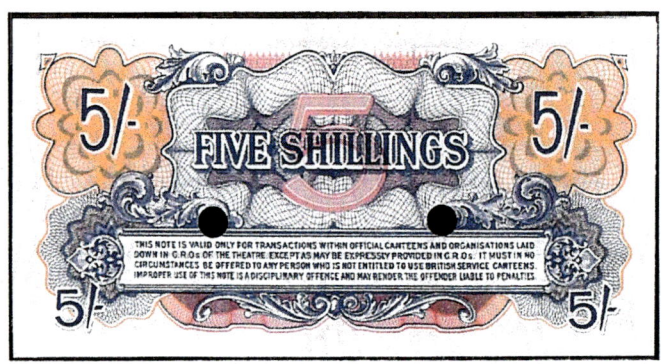

BRITISH ARMED FORCES · Second Series   29

RM 51 (PM21a) (E-20)   Ten Shillings
139 x 70mm · Green (Orange/Olive tints)
Security thread · Numbered in Black (centre right and bottom left)

RM 52 (PM21b) (E-27)
as RM51 but on watermarked paper · no thread

		V.F.	E.F.	Unc.
RM 51		£4	£8	£16
51b	S & B list punch cancel, Pick doesn't	- -	- -	- -
52	On watermarked paper · no thread	£3	£6	£12
52b	S & B list punch cancel, Pick doesn't	- -	- -	- -
52s	Specimen · guesstimate	- -	- -	£250

BRITISH ARMED FORCES · Second Series

RM 53 (PM22a) (E-21)　　　　　　　　　　　　One Pound
138 x 69/70mm · Purple (Red/Blue tints)
Security thread · Numbered (black) centre right and bottom left

RM 54 (PM20b) (SwB427b)
as RM53 but watermarked paper · no thread
Numbered in Black

		E.F.	Unc.
RM 53	Now readily available	- -	£1
Prefix AA/5 has been found printed on both 'normal' and a thicker paper. Although a very small difference the thread is not visible (it usually is) when note laid flat.		- -	- -
RM 54	On watermarked paper · guesstimate	- -	£15
54s	Specimen · (noted 1999) "Unc."	- -	£350
54s	Specimen · (noted 2001) "EF+"	- -	£450

BRITISH ARMED FORCES · Second Series   31

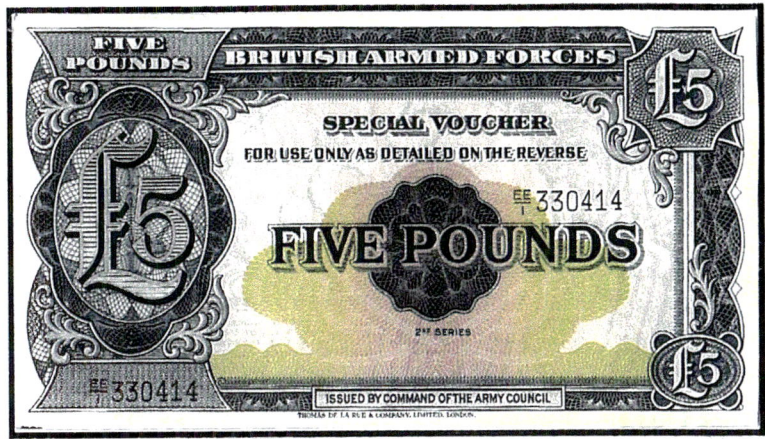

RM 55 (PM23) (E-28)   Five Pounds
149 x 80mm · Dark Blue (Olive/"Peach" tints)
Watermarked paper · Numbered in Black (centre right and bottom left)
The only special voucher to be partly printed intaglio
(engraved) and a rather splendid example of that art.

		E.F.	Unc.
RM 55a	Readily available	- -	£4
RM 55b	A uniface proof (intaglio part only) of front	- -	- -
RM 55s	Specimen · Schwann & Boling (dollars)	- -	$125

RM 56 part printed set 6d, 1/-, 2/6d, 5/-, 10/- and £1 Suez o/p £1,500
RM 56s   as above, a proof without the Suez overprint   £2,000

32 BRITISH ARMED FORCES · Third Series

Tokens: see page 15 for RMT 15 Half-unit and RMT 16 One Unit
Plates by De La Rue · Printing by John Waddington

Three Pence
114 x 57mm
Green
(Orange/Pink tints)
No number
Security Thread
Design as shown

RM 61 (PM24) (E-29)
Back similar to RM 62

	Imp.	V.F.	E.F.	Unc.
RM 61		£30	£60	£90
(noted 1998) "Fine+"	£60	---	---	
RM 61s specimen	---	---	---	

Six Pence
114 x 57mm
Lilac (Green tints)
Security Thread
No number

RM 62 (PM25) (E-30)

	V.F.	E.F.	Unc.
RM 62	£20	£60	£90
RM 62s specimen			---

BRITISH ARMED FORCES · Third Series 33

One Shilling
114 x 57mm
Blue
(Pink / Brown tints)
No number
Security Thread

RM 63 (PM26a) (E-31)

RM 63b (PM26b)

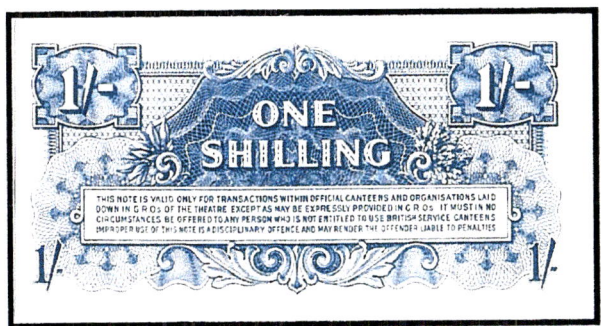

BACK common to all (disregarding holes)	V.F.	E.F.	Unc.
RM 63a uncancelled	£12	£20	£40
RM 63b cancelled · 2 holes	- - -	£5	£10
RM 63s specimen · 1 hole	- - -	£25	- - -

34 BRITISH ARMED FORCES · Third Series

RM 64 (PM26A) (E-32)   Two Shillings Sixpence
2/6d · Green and Red · 126 x 63mm · Back similar to RM 65

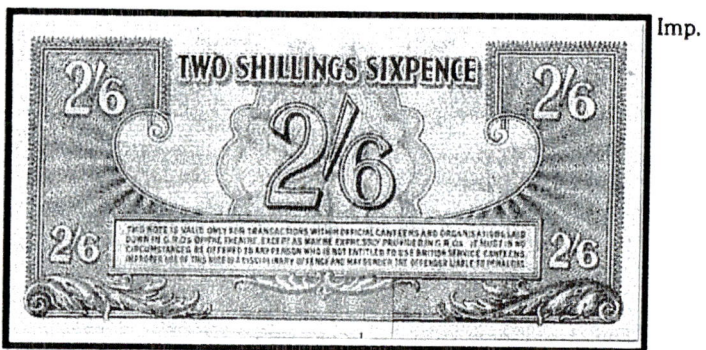

		Fine	V.F.	E.F.	Unc.
RM 64a	(noted 1997)	£100	---	---	---
RM 64s	specimen	---	---	£250	---

BRITISH ARMED FORCES · Third Series   35

RM 65 (PM27) (E-33)   Five Shillings
5/- · Orange (Blue '5', Green tints) · 126 x 63mm
Security thread · Numbered once at right

		Fine	V.F.	E.F.	Unc.
RM 65	(noted 1995) "Fine/V.F."	---	£220	---	---
RM 65s	specimen (Phillips 1995)	---	£220	---	---

BRITISH ARMED FORCES · Third Series

RM 66 (PM28) (E-34) Ten Shillings
Numbered (black) centre right and bottom left
Rich Red (Green/Orange tints) · 139 x 70mm
Security thread

BACK showing punched cancellation of RM 66b

		Fine	V.F.	E.F.	Unc.
RM 66a	(noted 1997) · unpunched	---	---	---	£75
RM 66b	cancelled with two punched holes	---	---	£8	£25
RM 66s	specimen	---	---	---	---

BRITISH ARMED FORCES · Third Series

RM 67 (PM29) (E-35)   One Pound

Numbered (black) upper right and bottom left
Brown (Pink/Lilac tints) · 139 x 70mm
Security thread

BACK RM 67

		E.F.	Unc.
RM 67	now readily available	- - -	£1
RM 67	(noted 1998) "crisp unc."	- - -	£1.50
RM 67s	specimen (noted 2001) "E.F."	£400	- - - -

38　BRITISH ARMED FORCES · Fourth Series

Imp.

RM 68 (SB441) (E-36)　　　　　　　　Three Pence
Not numbered · not officially issued
Grey (Green tints) · 114 x 57mm · Security thread

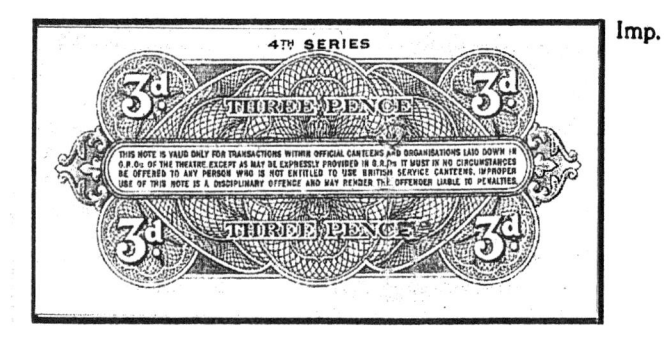

Imp.

BACK of RM 68

		E.F.	Unc.
RM 68	(Guesstimate)	---	£900
RM 68p	Uniface/black print (noted 1999)	---	£125
RM 68s	specimen punch cancelled · 1 hole	---	----

BRITISH ARMED FORCES · Fourth Series 39

Imp.

RM 69 (SB442) (E-37)   Six Pence
Not numbered · not officially issued
Blue (Violet and Green tints) · 114 x 57mm · Security thread

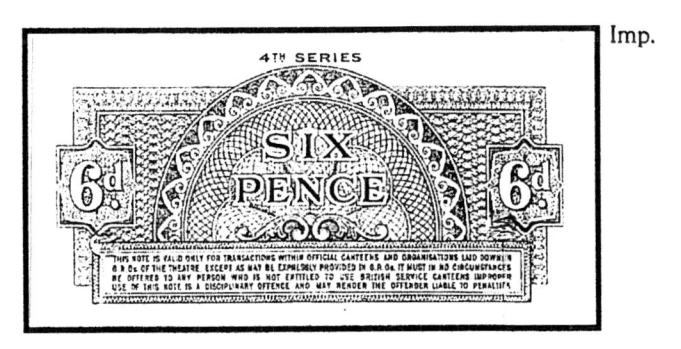

Imp.

BACK of RM 69

		E.F.	Unc.
RM 69	(Guesstimate)	---	£900
RM 69p	Uniface/black print (noted 1997)	---	£120
RM 69s	specimen · punch cancelled · 1 hole	---	----

BRITISH ARMED FORCES · Fourth Series

RM 70 (PM32a) (E-38) One Shilling
Not numbered · not officially issued
Brown (Orange and Olive tints) · 114 x 57mm
Security thread

BACK showing punched cancellation of RM 70b

		E.F.	Unc.
RM 70	Uncancelled (noted 1994)	- - -	£50
RM 70	Uncancelled (noted 1999)	- - -	£75
RM 70b	Punch cancelled 2 holes	- - -	£8
RM 70s	Specimen, punch cancelled 1 hole	£60	£95

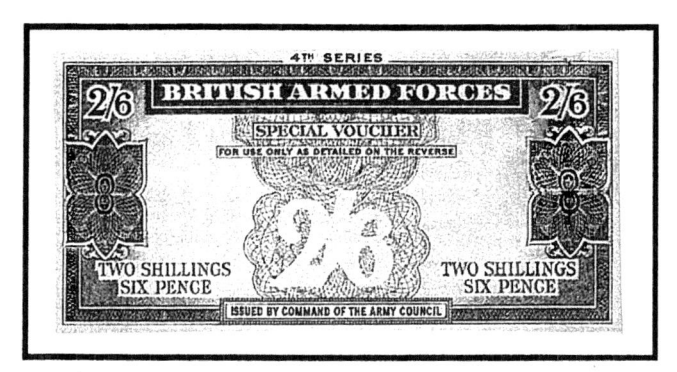

BRITISH ARMED FORCES · Fourth Series 41

Imp.

RM 71 (PM33) (E-39) Two Shillings Sixpence
Not officially issued · numbered prefix N
Reddish Orange (Violet and Green tints) · 126 x 63mm
Security thread

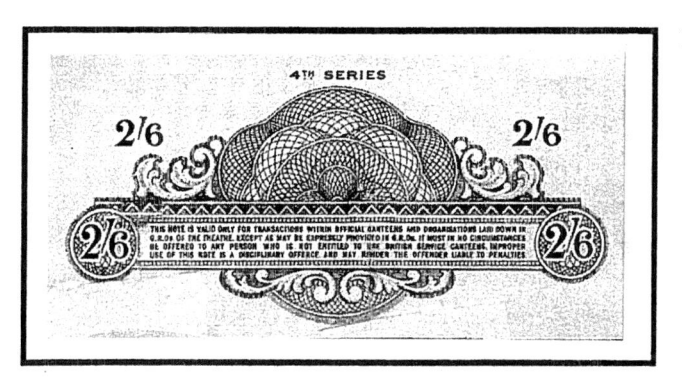

Imp.

BACK of RM 71

		E.F.	Unc.
RM 71	(Guesstimate)	---	£1000
RM 71s	specimen · punch cancelled · 1 hole	---	-----

42   BRITISH ARMED FORCES · Fourth Series

Imp.

RM 72 (SB445) (E-40) Five Shillings
Not officially issued · numbered prefix M
Green (Brown tints) · 126 x 63mm
Security thread

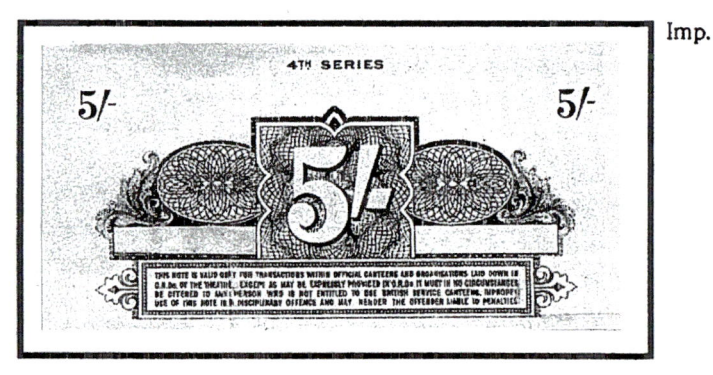

Imp.

BACK RM 72

		E.F.	Unc.
RM 72		- - -	- - - -
RM 72s	Specimen · punch cancelled · 1 hole	- - -	£950

BRITISH ARMED FORCES · Fourth Series 43

RM 73 (SB446) (E-41)   Ten Shillings
Numbered bottom left and upper right · security thread
Purple (Blue and Green tints) · 138 x 70mm

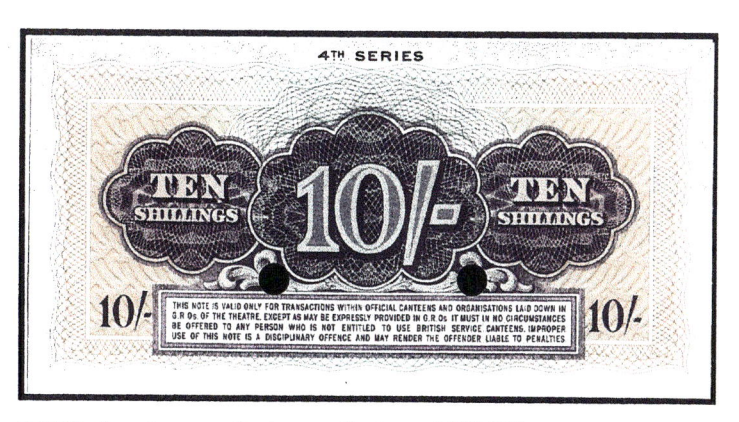

BACK showing punched cancellation of RM 73b

			V.F.	E.F.	Unc.
RM 73	(noted 1999)		£5	£20	£75
RM 73p	Proof showing position of secret marks	- - -	- - -	£250
RM 73b	Punched 1 hole		- - -	- - -	£80
RM 73c	Punched 2 holes		- - -	- - -	£5
RM 73s	specimen · punch cancelled · 1 hole	- - -	- - -	- - - -

BRITISH ARMED FORCES · Fourth Series

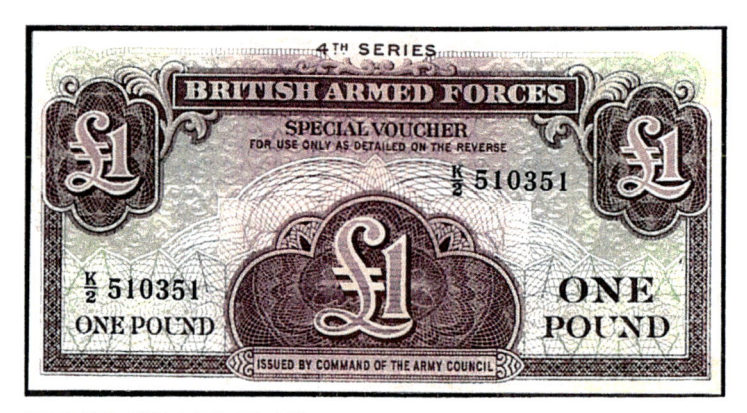

RM 74 (SB447) (E-42)   One Pound

Numbered bottom left and upper right · security thread
Brownish Purple (Lilac and Green tints) · 138 x 70mm

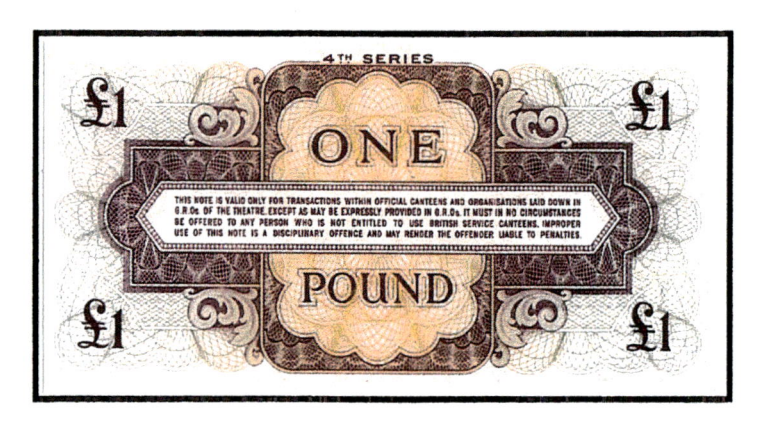

BACK RM74

		V.F.	E.F.	Unc.
RM 74	(noted 1999)	---		£1
RM 74p	Uniface proof/black (at auction 1998)	---	---	£125
RM 74s	specimen · punched 1 hole	---	---	£200

BRITISH ARMED FORCES · "Extras"   45

First Series · RM 28s · with De La Rue Oval Stamp

First Series · RM 30s · with De La Rue Oval Stamp

Second Series · RM 54s · with De La Rue Oval Stamp

BRITISH ARMED FORCES · Fifth Series

RM 80 (SB451s) (E-43) Three Pence
It is thought that there are only proofs and essays
Reddish Brown (Purple and Grey tints) · 114 x 57mm

BACK of RM80

		V.F.	E.F.	Unc.
RM 80	Unpunched proof/ essay	---	---	---
RM 80s	Punch cancelled 2 holes	---	---	£950

BRITISH ARMED FORCES · Fifth Series

Imp.

RM 81 (SB452s) (E-44)　　　　　Six Pence
It is thought that there are only proofs and essays
Green (Turquoise and Brown tints) · 114 x 57mm

Imp.

BACK of RM81

		V.F.	E.F.	Unc.
RM 81	Unpunched proof/ essay	- - -	- - -	- - -
RM 81s	Punch cancelled 2 holes	- - -	- - -	£900

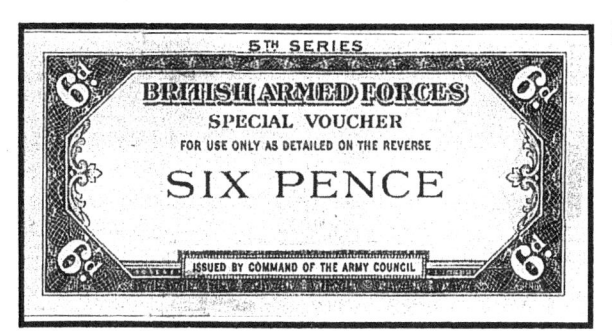

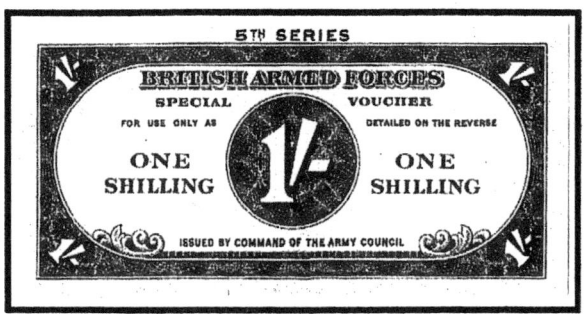

48 BRITISH ARMED FORCES · Fifth Series

Imp.

RM 82 (SB453s) (E-45)   One Shilling
It is thought that there are only proofs and essays
Lilac (Green tints) · 114 x 57mm

Imp.

BACK of RM82

		V.F.	E.F.	Unc.
RM 82	Unpunched proof/ essay	- - -	- - -	- - -
RM 82p	Uniface proofs, black, front and back	- - -	- - -	£250
RM 82s	Punch cancelled 2 holes	- - -	- - -	£950

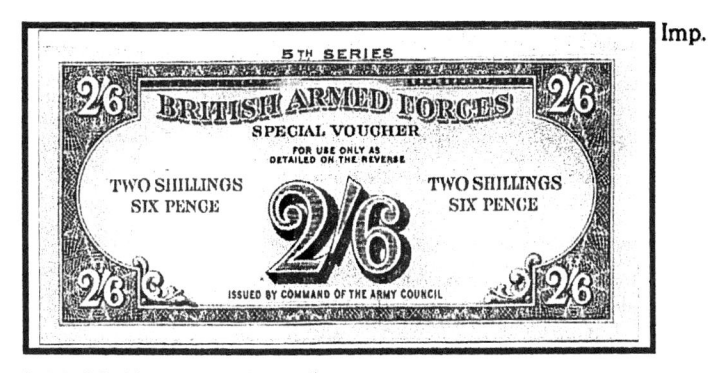

BRITISH ARMED FORCES · Fifth Series 49

Imp.

RM 83 (SB454s) (E-46)   Two Shillings Sixpence
It is thought that there are only proofs and essays
Purple (Turquoise and Brown tints) · 126 x 63mm
No number to RM 83
RM 83s numbered upper right: $\frac{S}{1}$ 123456

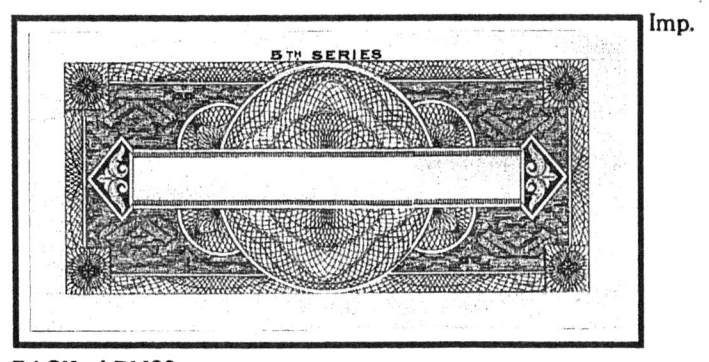

Imp.

BACK of RM83

		V.F.	E.F.	Unc.
RM 83	Unpunched proof / essay	- - -	- - -	- - -
RM 83p	Uniface proof / black	- - -	£100	- - -
RM 83s	Numbered and punch cancelled 2 holes	- - -	- - -	£900

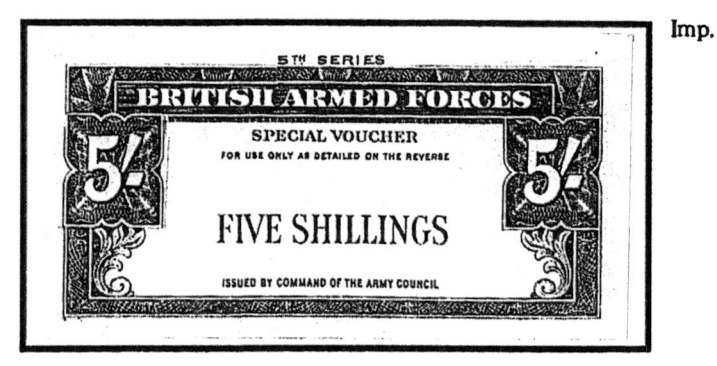

BRITISH ARMED FORCES · Fifth Series

Imp.

RM 84 (SB455s) (E-47) Five Shillings
It is thought that there are only proofs and essays
Blue (Red and Turquoise tints) · 126 x 63mm
No number to RM 84
RM 84s numbered upper right $\frac{R}{1}$ 123456

Imp.

BACK of RM84

		V.F.	E.F.	Unc.
RM 84	Unpunched proof/ essay	---	---	---
RM 84p	Uniface proofs, black	---	£100	---
RM 84p2	Uniface proofs, black · design variation	---	£100	---
RM 84s	Numbered and punch cancelled 2 holes	---	---	£900

BRITISH ARMED FORCES · Fifth Series 51

Imp.

RM 85 (SB456s) (E-48) Ten Shillings

It is thought that there are only proofs and essays
Orange (Green and Grey tints) · 140 x 69mm
No number to RM 85

RM 85s numbered left and right, $\frac{Q}{1}$ 123456 or $\frac{Q}{1}$ 789012

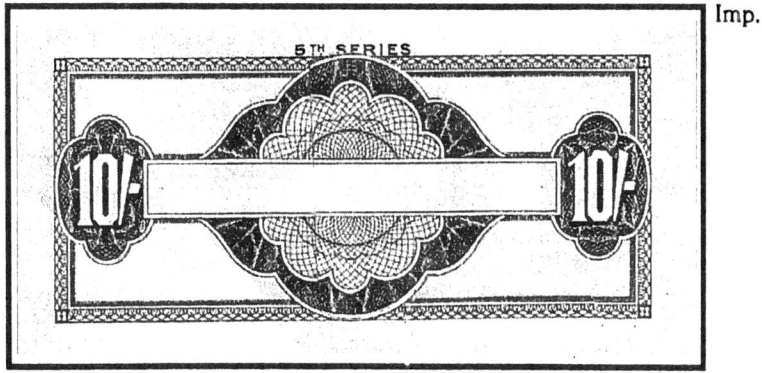

Imp.

BACK of RM85

		V.F.	E.F.	Unc.
RM 85	Unpunched proof/ essay	- - -	- - -	- - -
RM 85p	Uniface proof/black	- - -	£100	- - -
RM 85s	Numbered and punch cancelled 2 holes	- - -	- - -	£900

BRITISH ARMED FORCES · Fifth Series

RM 86 (SB457s) (E-49)   One Pound

It is thought that there are only proofs and essays
Olive (Red and Brown tints) · 140 x 69mm
No number to RM 86
RM 86s numbered left and right $\frac{P}{1}$ 123456   or $\frac{P}{1}$ 789012

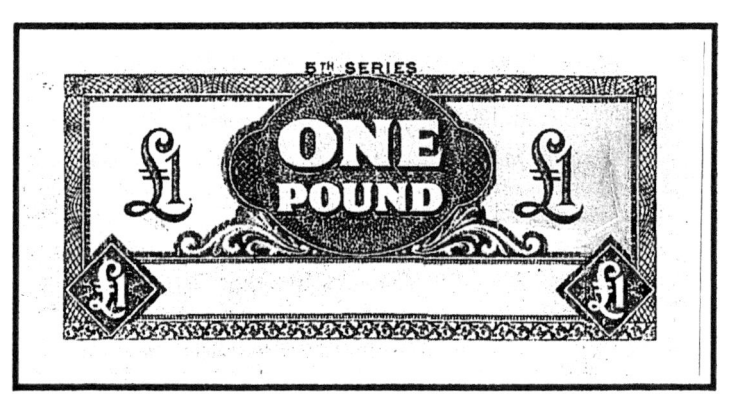

BACK of RM86

	V.F.	E.F.	Unc.
RM 86 Unpunched proof/ essay	---	---	---
RM 86p Uniface proofs, black	---	---	---
RM 86s Numbered and punch cancelled 2 holes	---	---	£900

BRITISH ARMED FORCES · "Extras" 53

RM 56e · One of a number of essays for the Second Series

Third Series · RM 65s2 with De La Rue Oval Stamp

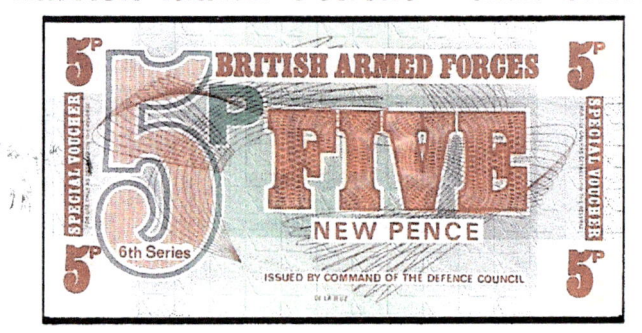

54 BRITISH ARMED FORCES · Sixth Series

RM90 (SB458a)(E-50)   Five New Pence
wavy line watermark
Brown and Green · 114 x 57mm · De La Rue
De La Rue fronts have feint "tiled" effect

RM91 (SB458b)(E-53)   Five New Pence
wavy line watermark
Brown and Green · 114 x 57mm · Bradbury Wilkinson

	Unc.
RM90	50p
RM91	75p

(noted 1996)
At auction specimen set:
5p, 10p, 50p   £140

Back, common to both

BRITISH ARMED FORCES · Sixth Series 55

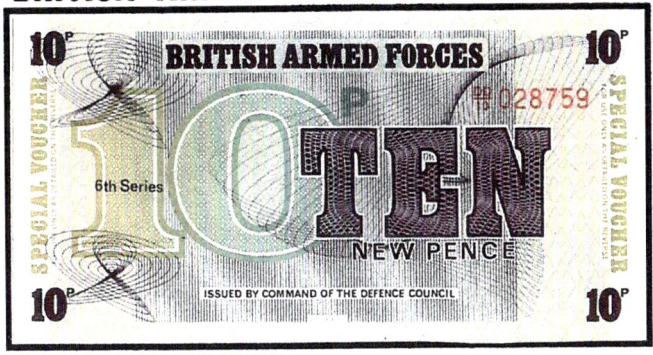

RM92 (SB459a)(E-51)   Ten New Pence
wavy line watermark · De La Rue
Purple (Olive and Green tints) · 127 x 63mm · numbered prefix: $\frac{DD}{10}$

RM93 (SB459b)(E-54) wavy line w/mark   Ten New Pence
Purple (Olive and Green tints) · 127 x 63mm · Bradbury Wilkinson · prefix: $\frac{A}{1}$ to $\frac{A}{6}$
Feint pattern quite different as clearly seen in large, front 10 p

	Unc.
RM92	50p
RM93	75p

Back, common to both

56 BRITISH ARMED FORCES · Sixth Series

RM94 (SB460a)(E-52) 140 x 70mm Fifty New Pence
Geen (Pink tints) · watermarked · De La Rue · prefix: $\frac{BB}{10}$

RM95 (SB460b)(E-55) Bradbury Wilkinson · prefix $\frac{B}{1}$ & $\frac{B}{2}$

	Unc.
RM99	75p
RM100	75p

Feint pattern quite different as clearly seen in large, back 50p